500
DAD
JOKES

PUNS, ONE-LINERS
& WORDPLAY

LOWELL FISHER

THESE ARE DAD JOKES.

BAD DAD JOKES.

THEY ARE

DAD TESTED.

DAD VOTED.

DAD APPROVED.

IF YOU ARE A DAD, ENJOY.

IF YOU AREN'T DAD,
YOU'VE BEEN WARNED.

Where do they write about dead planets?
The orbit-uary!

What is the definition of an acorn?
In a nutshell, an oak tree.

Why don't your mom's sisters ever get sick?
They have auntie bodies.

What do you call an organization that donates places to sit?
A chair-ity.

What drink always has a cold?
Cough-ee.

What do you call a bacon-wrapped dinosaur?
Jurassic Pork.

What tree has the sniffles all the time?
A sycamore.

I told my 14 year-old son I thought "Fortnite" was a silly name for a computer game.
I think it's just two week.

What is the difference between a nicely dressed man on a tricycle and a poorly dressed man on a bicycle?
A tire.

I recently ate at a restaurant where they charge you for bad manners.
I guess that's what you call *fine* dining!

Marriage has its pros and cons.
On one hand you get to wear a ring, on the other you don't.

If pronouncing my b's as v's makes me sound Russian, **then Soviet.**

A young boy felt bad after he accidentally let the neighbor's cat loose. After two weeks, the missing cat seemed to be gone for good. "I'm very sorry," the boy told the neighbor. "I'd like to replace your cat for you." "O.K.," the neighbor said, **"How good are you at catching mice?"**

One night I was lying in bed, looking up at the stars, and thought to myself, **"My roof is gone!"**

How does Moses make his tea?
Hebrews it.

I just ate bread from the worst bakery in America.
I'd take you there, but there's no knead.

A kid just threw milk, cream and butter at my car.
How dairy!

Did you hear about the clarinetist who played in tune?
Neither did I.

How did the yak almost die?
Cardi-yak arrest.

Two guys were about to get into a fight. One draws a line in the dirt and says, "If you cross this line, I'll hit you in the mouth."
That was the punch line.

My grandfather died because the report said he had type A blood.
Actually, it was a type O.

Here's something you might not have known about me, I can cut wood by just looking at it. It's true!
I saw it with my own eyes.

My wife said, "Don't get upset if someone calls you fat."
"You're much bigger than that!"

What did the shy ear of corn say after he was complimented?
"Awwwwww, shucks!"

I asked my friend, Rick, if he had five cents I could borrow.
But he was Nicholas.

What's the best pickup line?
A fishing line.

I know many of you are sad because it's a Monday.
But don't forget, only 48 hours ago, it was a sadder day.

Did you hear about the guy who was in the water but said he wasn't?
He was in the Nile.

I feel bad for deep-sea divers.
They really have a lot of pressure on them.

What's the definition of a will?
It's a dead giveaway.

Why did Little Miss Muffet push
Humpty Dumpty off the wall?
He got in her whey!

Why did Stalin only write in lowercase?
He was afraid of capitalism.

How many ears does Spock have?
**Three: the left ear, the right ear, and
the final frontier.**

Why can't kids tell dad jokes?
They're not fully groan.

Bread is like the sun -- rises in the yeast **and sets in the waist.**

I just found out my friend has a secret life as a priest.
It's his altar ego.

Rest in peace boiling water,
you will be mist.

I mustache you a question.
Never mind, I'll shave it for later.

What should you do if there are 14 frogs on your car's back window?
Use your rear window de-frogger.

What do cloves use for money?
Garlic bread.

Why don't computer programmers like nature?
It has way too many bugs.

I was surprised to learn there was a place called Jerusalem.
But, Israel.

The world tongue-twister champion just got arrested.
I hear they're going to give him a really tough sentence.

What do you call caged hens stacked upon one another?
Layers.

What do you call a school that specializes in teaching nuts?
Macadamia.

I just got a bad electric shock!
I'm O.K., it just Hertz.

There are no favorites in the Puppy Bowl.
Only underdogs.

My parents told me the world didn't revolve around me.
"But I'm your son," I said!

Did you hear about the artist who paints in jail?
He had a brush with the law.

How much does it cost to buy a big boat?
A yacht.

Did you know you can bring your dog to the bank with you?
They're just not allowed to make deposits.

Did you hear about the light bulb party?
It was pretty lit!

What do you call the president of a waterproof clothing company?
The head poncho.

What do cows tell each other at bedtime?
Dairy tales.

What did the Iraqi daughter say when she got her birthday present?
"Thanks for the Baghdad!"

What's the hardest part about learning inline skating?
The ground!

Why did the chicken cross the road, roll in the mud, and cross the road again?
Because he was a dirty double-crosser.

Did you hear about the nun who didn't do her laundry?
She had a filthy habit.

I have a friend from Prague who I like to play chess with.
He's my Czech mate.

In what state can you see a priest sneeze and then sit down?
Massachusetts.

Did you hear about the mosquito who became a comedian?
People think he's malarious.

If you are intimidated by a date, remember one thing,
they are just dried up plums.

What did one pumpkin say to the other?
"Well, hello there, gourd-geous!"

Puns about communism aren't funny **unless everyone gets them.**

Scientists got bored watching the earth turn, **so after 24 hours they called it a day.**

What do camels use to hide themselves?
Camel-flage.

Why is "beefstew" a bad password?
It's not stroganoff.

Why don't all couples go to the gym together?
Because some relationships just don't work out.

Why did the old man fall down the well?
He couldn't see that well!

Why don't aliens visit our solar system?
Bad ratings. Only one star.

I wanted to get a band aid tattoo,
but I was afraid I couldn't pull it off.

I love politically incorrect jokes. Here's my favorite: **Benjamin Franklin was a great president!**

I don't mind you checking books out of the library.
Just try not to overdue, it O.K.?

David Hasselhoff has started to just refer to himself as Hoff.
It's just less of a hassle.

Today, my son asked "Can I have a bookmark?" and I burst into tears. Ten years old and **he still doesn't know my name is Steve.**

Did you hear about the bee that was overweight?
It had chub-bee legs and a flab-bee body.

What happened when the pig fell off his horse?
He got bay-con, of course.

How do you know how heavy a red hot chili pepper is?
Give it a weigh, give it a weigh, give it a weigh now!

What do you get if you cross a centipede and a parrot?
A walkie-talkie.

What kind of songs do the planets sing? **Nep-tunes!**

Yesterday, I crossed a road, changed a light bulb and walked into a bar.
My life is turning into a joke.

Son: I almost fell down the stairs with a basket of laundry. It was a close one!
Dad: Don't you mean a *clothes* one?"

What do you call a guy who takes his girlfriend to an ice rink with a half-priced ticket?
A cheapskate.

Mountains aren't just funny,
they're also hill areas.

I have this great joke about amnesia,
but I forgot how it goes.

Aunt: I need to go and feed my baby hamsters.
Dad: **Are you sure your baby will like them?**

Why did the printer stop making music?
It ran out of toner.

Where do belly buttons go to college?
The Naval Academy.

Why do chemists like nitrates so much?
Because they're cheaper than day rates.

My wife complains that I never buy her flowers.
But I never knew she was selling any!

What do you mean June is over?
Julying.

Why did the man quit his job at the cement factory?
It just got harder and harder.

How did the intruder get into the garage?
In tru-da-window!

Why did the man only buy nine racquets?
'Cause tennis too many.

Finally my winter fat is gone and now
I just have spring rolls.

My son just lost his taste buds in a bad accident. I wanted to make a joke out of it, **but I think it would be tasteless.**

What do you get when you eat Christmas ornaments?
Tinsel-itis!

A pirate walks into a bar with a paper towel on his head. The bartender says, "What's with the paper towel?" The pirate says, **"Arrr... I've got a bounty on me head."**

What do you call a dog that does magic?
A labracadabrador.

What do you call illegal trafficking of carbon dioxide?
Smoggling.

I sympathize with batteries,
I'm never included in anything either.

What do you call someone who delivers Indian food?
A currier.

I just spent half an hour looking for scissors to open a package. When I told my wife she said,
"Oh honey, it's tearable."

I don't have a dad bod.
I have more of a father figure.

Someone stole my mirror yesterday. **They need to take a long hard look at themselves!**

I got my best friend a fridge for his birthday. I can't wait to see his face **light up when he opens it.**

Geology rocks but **astronomy is really far out.**

I just got a new job at a prison library. **It has its pros and cons.**

Free roofing. On the house.

Why do astronomers put beef in their shampoo?
Meatier showers.

What noise does a 747 make when it bounces?
Boeing, Boeing, Boeing!

What do you call an acid with an attitude?
A mean ole acid!

Policeman: I'm sorry to tell you this, but your son set the school on fire
Mom: Our son?
Dad: Yes, it's arson.

Why don't cows wear flip-flops?
They lactose!

Did you hear about the Spanish train robber?
He had loco motives!

How do you get a sea creature to play music?
You tuna fish.

Be careful what you do in college.
Bad things you will follow you, fraternity.

What's the difference between roast beef and pea soup?
Anyone can roast beef!

Did you hear about the clown who broke his arm?
It was humerus!

What do you call a man who can identify different types of flames?
A fire distinguisher!

My coworker called me selfish for reheating salmon in the microwave.
"But it's not shellfish!" I replied.

What happened to the man who wanted a brain transplant?
He changed his mind.

My twin brother said he didn't understand cloning.
That makes two of us.

What do you call a vegetable that helps direct a film?
A producer!

How do you resuscitate a sheep?
You give it Sheep-PR.

How much of an iceberg can you really see?
Seriously, any tips welcome.

How can you make money as a waiter?
Seriously, any tips welcome.

How can I get the wax out of my ears?
Seriously, any tips welcome.

I am really hungry for bits of meat stewed in gravy.
Seriously, any tips welcome.

I have a lot of jokes about unemployed people.
But none of them work.

Today I learned that Stephen King has a famous son named Joe.
I'm not joking, he is.

For my next trick, I will disappear.
Wow, this is the worst pear ever!
And you smell bad, pear!

Why are solos always so quiet?
Because they're so low.

I've started a business making boats in my attic.
Sails have been going through the roof!

Captain Hook is **single-handedly my favorite Disney villain.**

Have you heard the rumor about peanut butter? Oh sorry, I can't tell you. **You might spread it.**

Did you hear who won the 5K race in Bangkok?
It was a Thai.

What is a prisoner's favorite punctuation mark?
The period. It marks the end of a sentence.

Why do toadstools grow so close together?
They don't need mushroom.

Why is the word "dark" spelled with a "k" and not a "c"?
Because you can't see in the dark.

Why are bankers sad?
Because they're loan-ly.

There's something about subtraction
that just doesn't add up.

Was the man sad when his flashlight
batteries died?
No, he was delighted!

Why should you never talk about
infinity with a math geek?
They go on about it forever.

What do you say to your sister when she's crying?
"Are you having a cry, sis?"

Son: I've had the impression there's something wrong with this chair
Dad: Maybe you're just having a bad chair day.

"I'll have the turtle soup.
And make it snappy!"

I just figured out why Beyoncé's hair is always blowing in every picture--
all her fans!

What do you call an Italian Jedi?
Obi-Wan Cannoli.

What's more expensive, a ladder or a gold watch?
The latter.

I once started a business raising chickens,
but I struggled to make hens meat.

We can't take our dog outside anymore because the ducks keep attacking him.
Guess that's what we get for buying a purebred dog.

What type of dessert is always late to the party?
Choco-late.

I went to IKEA yesterday.
It was a Swede experience.

Dad: There's only one thing about Halloween that scares me.
Son: Which is…?
Dad: Exactly!

What's the best birthday present you could get?
A broken drum, you can't beat it.

Waiter: How did you find your meal, sir?
Dad: It wasn't too difficult, it was right on the plate!

What's blue and not really heavy at all?
Light blue.

Within minutes, the detective knew exactly what the murder weapon was.
It was a briefcase.

What did the nut say when chasing the other nut?
"I'm a cashew!"

Where do you keep Arnold Schwarzenegger action figures in a store?
"Aisle B...back!"

What types of people never get angry?
Nomads.

What do you call it when your feet fall asleep?
Coma-toes.

What did the drummer call his twin daughters?
Anna one, Anna two.

What do you call the other people that work in the Hibachi restaurant with you?
Co-wokers.

How many lumberjacks does it take to screw in a light bulb?
About tree fellers.

What do you say to a pickle that is freaking out?
"Just dill!"

Why was the printer playing music?
The paper was jamming.

What did the man who invented the
door knocker win?
A no-bell prize.

The army men were losing the battle
until they started throwing the tops of
kitchen cupboards.
It was a counter attack.

What do you call a fish with two knees?
A two-knee fish.

I've been diagnosed with a chronic
fear of giants.
It's called fee fi phobia.

What does a panda use to make pancakes?
A pan. Duh.

Do you like my new painting?
It's my claim to frame.

What's the derivative of Amazon?
Amazon Prime.

What do the Romans use to cut their pizza?
Little Caesars.

I was going to give archery a shot, **but is has too many drawbacks.**

It is weird to see signs that say "In case of fire, don't use elevator". Everyone knows that **water is waaaay better than an elevator to use to put out fires!**

To the man in the cast who stole my camouflage pants, **you can hide, but you can't run!**

I started a band called 999 megabytes. **We still haven't gotten a gig.**

My son keeps chewing on the live electric wires,
so I had to ground him.

I went into a crypt but I couldn't recognize the bodies.
I guess there were encrypted.

If a cow doesn't produce milk,
it's both an udder failure, and a milk dud.

Is an old rope good enough for tying things down?
Frayed knot.

My son made a dad joke about an axe.
But it just wasn't very cleaver.

Son: Dad, what gift should I give my
Dutch girlfriend?
Dad: I'd give her a clog...wooden
shoe?

Someone who tends to chickens
is a real-life chicken tender.

What did the sofa say when it got hurt?
"Couch!"

This is top secret...

This is bottom secret...

How many tickles does it take to make an octopus laugh?
Tentacles.

What did the thunder god have a lot of during puberty?
Thormones.

My coworkers are like Christmas lights.
Half of them don't work, and the other half aren't that bright

Did you know that atoms are Catholic?
Yep, they have mass.

Why was the pizzeria so slow?
The servers were down.

Why does Superman get invited to dinners?
Because he's a supper hero.

After you die, what part of your body is the last to stop working?
Your pupils, they dilate.

I got so mad at my wife when she told me I had no sense of direction.
So I packed up my things and right.

A car's weakest part is the **nut holding the steering wheel.**

My wife ripped the blankets off me last night!
But I shall recover.

How can you tell when a banker becomes bored?
He starts losing interest!

Why are Canadians the fiercest competitors of all time?
They always bring their "eh" game.

Did you ever meet my vegetarian girlfriend?
Because I don't think you met herbivore.

How do fish go to war?
In tanks!

What's the pope's favorite cheese?
Swiss, because it's holey!

What's the difference between a high baseball hit and a maggot's father?
One's a pop fly, the other's a fly's pop.

Two wind turbines are in a field. One asks the other,
"What's your favorite kind of music because I'm a huge metal fan."

A slice of apple pie is $2.50 in Jamaica and $3.00 in the Bahamas.
These, my friend, are the pie rates of the Caribbean.

What happened when the man's tortilla broke off into the salsa?
He abandoned chip.

All billboards communicate to us
using sign language

What do you call a nervous javelin thrower at a Renaissance fair?
Shakespeare.

Dad: I need to call the doctor today.
Son: Witch doctor?
Dad: No, the regular kind.

Why did Satan tear the shoe in half?
Cause he just wanted the sole.

Some people have commented that I smell like coins. I tell them **it's just my natural cent.**

If you drop an ice cube on the floor, just kick it under the refrigerator.
Soon, it will just be water under the fridge.

What do you call Chewbacca's pillow?
A Wookie-cushion!

What happens if the average number of bullies at a school goes up?
The mean increases.

Where do they put army babies?
In the infantry.

How many eyes does a cyclops have?
None, if you're spelling it correctly.

Why did the printer go to the gym?
To get toner.

The internet connection at my farm is
really sketchy, so I moved the modem
to the barn.
Now I have stable wi-fi.

What do you call a tree that can't figure
out a riddle?
Stumped.

In college, I tried to put my grades up for adoption.
Because I just couldn't raise them on my own.

What kind of gator gives the best directions?
A navi-gator.

What do you call a man who can't stand?
Neil.

What vegetable do plumbers hate?
Leeks.

Why did Sherlock Holmes eat at the Mexican Restaurant?
He wanted a good case idea.

Boss: How good are you at PowerPoint?
Dad: I Excel at it.
Boss: Was that a pun?
Dad: Word.

Is it just me or are circles kind of **pointless?**

I remember the first time I got a universal remote.
I thought, "This changes everything!"

We should have known communism wouldn't work -- **too many red flags!**

My mom was a 10K runner, and my dad was a marathon runner.
It was a mixed-race marriage.

Did you hear about the red ship and the blue ship that collided?
Both crews were marooned!

What does E.T. stand for?
Mostly when he wants to walk somewhere.

Why is Sunday stronger than Monday?
Because Monday is a weekday.

What's the difference between ignorance and apathy?
I don't know and I don't care.

I mixed up two letters in my dad joke.
And now the whole thing is urined.

What's a bodybuilder's favorite drink?
A proteini.

Why couldn't the leopard creep up on his prey?
He was spotted.

Someone once told me that their dog could retrieve a ball from up to a mile away.
It seems a bit far-fetched to me.

Why did the man get arrested at the grocery store?
Disturbing the peas.

How do monsters like their eggs?
Terri-fried.

You want to hear a joke about someone who never goes outdoors? Actually, you wouldn't get it. **It's an inside joke.**

Why are tigers always honest? **Because they aren't lion.**

What do you call a row of people lifting a block of cheddar? **A cheesy pickup line.**

You know you have a severe iron deficiency **when your shirt is all wrinkled.**

I used to have a fear of hurdles,
but I got over them.

Did you hear the story about the frog?
It was ribbitting.

As I handed my dad his 40th birthday card, he looked at me with tears in his eyes and said…
"You know, one would have been plenty."

How did I get out of Iraq?
Iran!

My friend keeps saying, "Cheer up man, it could be worse, you could be stuck underground in a hole full of water"
I know he means well.

What did the grape say when it got stepped on?
Nothing, it just let out a little whine.

What do you call a man with 10 ants?
A landlord.

How does the man in the moon cut his hair?
Eclipse it.

How do locomotives know where to go?
Lots of training.

Do we dream in color, **or is it just a pigment of our imagination?**

What did one tectonic plate say to the other after an earthquake?
"My fault."

Has anyone checked on Oklahoma recently?
Are they still OK?

My son hated going to jail. He got mad at everyone, refused to eat and lay in bed all day.
After that, we never played Monopoly again.

How do chickens motivate their kids?
They egg them on.

The inventor of the throat lozenge has died.
There will be no coffin at his funeral.

What do you call a fist bump in the United Kingdom?
A British pound.

Dad: Hey, they're stopping all the airplanes at the airport?
Son: What! Why?
Dad: To let people get off.

My son was looking for books on dinosaurs. So I asked the librarian to suggest a good author.
"Try Sarah Topps," she said.

My friend told me to stop acting like a flamingo **so I had to put my foot down.**

How did the dog make antifreeze?
He ran off with her blanket!

I knew a guy who collected Altoids.
They were all in mint condition.

Why do hipsters only use the
microwave?
They don't like conventional ovens.

What is the TSA called in Canada?
TS, eh?

A lumberjack went into a forest to cut a tree. He started to swing at the tree, when the tree shouted, "Wait! I'm a talking tree!"
The lumberjack replied, **"And you shall dialogue."**

My wife just bought me a chicken and an egg off Amazon.
I'll let you know which comes first.

What do you call a cow that is experiencing something from the past?
Deja moo.

A limbo player walks into a bar **and is immediately disqualified.**

Son, if I hear you slam the doors one more time, I'll be really upset. **You know I'm a huge Jim Morrison fan**.

Why did the jalapeño ask for the window to be closed? **He was a little chilly.**

Earlier today, a man released all the dogs from the dog kennel. **Police are desperately looking for leads**.

What do you call a woman standing in the middle of a tennis court?
Annette.

I gave up my seat to a blind person on the bus.
And that, my friend, is how I lost my job as bus driver!

My daughter yelled, "Daaaaaad, you haven't listened to one word I've said, have you!?"
"What a strange way to start a conversation," I thought.

Did you hear about the guy who's whole left side was cut off?
He's all right now.

Where can you find tastey Mentos?
On tastey men feet.

Why should you never throw away an old dolphin?
Because they can easily be re-porpoised.

What do you call a colorful dad?
A hueman.

I don't usually make bad puns about fractions.
But I will if I halve two.

My wife tripped and dropped the basket of clothes she had just ironed.
I sat there and watched it all unfold.

Why is your nose in the middle of your face?
Because it's the scenter.

What is the strongest cereal brand?
Shredded wheat.

What do you call a bee from America?
A USB.

What is a pirate's favorite drink?
High Sea.

What's Justin Timberlake's favorite part
of the Ukraine?
The Crimea River.

What types of explorers never seem to
get angry?
Nomads.

I never refuse pi.
That would be irrational.

My wife refuses to go karaokeing with
me **so I have to duet alone!**

How do you get down from an
elephant?
**You don't, you get down from a
goose.**

What do you call bears with no ears?
B.

The only thing The Flat Earth Society has to fear **is sphere itself.**

Who was the roundest knight at King Arthur's round table?
Sir Cumference.

If procrastination was an Olympic sport, **I would participate in the next one.**

My son swallowed some coins and was taken to a hospital. When I asked how he was the nurse said,
"No change yet!"

My wife told me I had to stop pretending to be butter.
But I can't, I'm on a roll!

I had a dream I weighed less than a thousandth of a gram.
I was like 0mg.

Did you hear about the crocodile who became a lawyer?
He was an expert dele-gator.

What does Pac-Man eat with his chips?
Guaca-waka-waka-mole.

My dog's been pretty upset ever since I switched him to an all-fruit diet. You could say he's a **little melon collie now.**

What do you call an ostrich that practices magic?
An ost-witch.

To be frank....**I'd have to change my name.**

What do you call a shirt with stalks of corn coming out it?
A crop top.

The Queen just knighted the first cow in history.
His name is Sir Loin.

Do cannibals eat ramen?
Or do they cook them first?

How warm was Luke Skywalker inside his Tauntaun?
Lukewarm.

Small babies may be delivered by a stork, **but larger ones are delivered by a crane**.

What relative looks like a fish?
Aunt Chovy.

What type of magazine do cows read?
Cattle-logs.

What do you call a South American woman who is always in a hurry?
Urgent Tina.

I accidentally handed my wife a glue stick instead of Chapstick.
She still isn't talking to me.

Statistically six out of seven dwarfs
aren't happy.

Did you hear about the shark attack?
It was fishious.

I really want a camouflage shirt,
but I can never find one.

Dad: Sorry sir, I can't come in today. I
have a wee cough.
Boss: You have a wee cough?
Dad: Really? Thanks see you next
week!

With great power comes **a huge electricity bill.**

If Americans switched from pounds to kilograms overnight, **there would be mass confusion.**

A toolbox only needs a single tool.
That's awl.

Who was the most famous car maker in Norway?
Henry Fjord.

I removed the shell from my favorite racing snail thinking it would make him faster. **But it's actually made him more sluggish.**

I was going to start a bourbon company, **but I heard it's really a whiskey business.**

How does Darth Vader like his toast? **On the dark side.**

No, I don't know what the word "apocalypse" means, but it's not like it's **the end of the world!**

Of all the inventions of the last 100 years, the dry-erase board **has to be the most remarkable.**

What kind of place puts you in handcuffs you when you sit down to eat?
A restaurant.

I got an email that read, "At Google Earth, we can read maps backwards!" and I thought, "**That's just spam!**"

How many bones are in the human hand?
Only a handful.

A blacksmith took a bet to see if he could spend three nights in a haunted house. He lost when he got scared and **made a bolt for the door.**

My wife asked if our kids were spoiled. I said, **"I think most kids smell that way."**

I've always wanted to be a parachute instructor. **So, I pulled a few strings.**

A thousand years ago, the boomerang was Australia's main export. **And import.**

Why couldn't the computer take its hat off?
Because it had its Caps Lock on.

What's a sloucher's favorite herb?
Slantro.

My son wanted to get a pet spider from the pet store, but they are really expensive.
I told him we can get a cheaper one off the web.

I wanted to be an accountant?
Because it's accrual world.

I walked into the biology lab, and saw my lab partner dissecting an insect.
"Your fly is open," I said.

Why didn't the man look for his missing watch?
He couldn't find the time.

Where do cows go for lunch?
The calf-eteria.

I think Santa lives in Brazil.
Last year, all my presents were from Amazon.

I have kleptomania, but when it gets really bad, **I take something for it.**

I like to tell dad jokes, but I don't have any kids. **I guess I'm a faux pa.**

How do you know when your cat is sick?
When it's not feline well.

What did the pirate say on his 80th birthday?
"Aye matey!"

What do pessimists and people who have a phobia of sausages have in common?
They both fear the worst!

What do you get when you throw a piano down a mineshaft?
A-flat minor.

Our can opener is broken
It's now a can't opener.

What's worst thing about driving for Uber?
All those people talking behind your back!

What do dogs get after they finish obedience school?
Their masters.

Did you hear the jokes about the undelivered letters?
No one seems to get them.

How do you know the man with the broken leg was in the movie?
He was in the cast.

I'm bad with four things...
face, names, and numbers.

What is the difference between a crocodile and an alligator?
One will see you later and the other will see you in a while.

Why were the police called to the daycare?
A two year-old was resisting a rest.

When I was a kid, you could walk into a store with two dollars and walk out with a gallon of milk, a dozen eggs and a loaf of bread. **But today they have cameras everywhere.**

Unfortunately, my obese parrot just died.
But it was a huge weight off my shoulders.

Next time your wife is angry, give her a towel as cape.
Then say, "Now you are super angry!"
She might laugh.
You might die.

Shout out to anyone who doesn't know **what the opposite of in is.**

You know what happened to the guy who chugged eight Cokes at once?
He burped 7 Up.

How can you find Will Smith in the snow?
Look for the fresh prints.

My dad always told me, "Don't be too quick to find faults."
Guess that's why he was a terrible geologist.

I got a job working in a hayfield.
After one day, I bailed.

Why did the pig stop sunbathing?
He was bacon in the heat.

I can always tell when someone is lying. **I can also tell when they're standing.**

I'm so upset! Someone stole my limbo stick!
How low can you go?

Why did the coffee go to the police?
It got mugged.

What do you call a smelly sheep?
A "P-ewe."

Lancelot and King Arthur are checking into a motel. Lancelot says, **"We'd like a room for two knights, please."**

Why can't T-Rexes clap their hands?
Because they're extinct.

A man walks into a bar with a piece of asphalt under his arm and asks the barman to make him a drink **and one for the road.**

How did the grizzly catch the fish?
With his bear hands.

Why was Pavlov's hair soft?
Because he conditioned it.

If you rearrange the letters of postmen,
they get really mad.

Why should you always split a taxi cab
fee?
It's only fare.

A weasel walks into a bar. The bartender says, "Wow, I've never served a weasel before, what can I get you?"
"Pop," goes the weasel.

It takes guts to be an **organ donor**

Why do all hot dogs look the same?
Because they're in-bread.

What do you call the president of Old MacDonald's farm?
The C-I-E-I-O.

I got fired from my job as a taxi driver. Turns out customers don't appreciate it **when you go the extra mile.**

I thought I won the argument with my wife as to how to arrange the furniture, but **the tables had turned.**

I was accused of burying clues in the cement, but **they had no concrete evidence.**

How do snakes separate bath towels? **Hiss and hers.**

Did you hear about the chicken who could only lay eggs in the winter? **She wasn't a spring chicken.**

Does my towel have a sense of humor? **Yeah, it's just really dry.**

I used to hate facial hair but then **it grew on me.**

How do know when a wedding is an emotional one? **Even the cake is in tiers.**

"Imprisonment" is more than just a word,
it's a sentence.

You can't plant flowers
if you haven't botany.

A man is washing his car with his son.
The son says,
"Dad can you just use a sponge?"

I'm never again donating money to anyone collecting for a marathon.
They just take the money and run.

Why can't a bicycle stand on its own?
Because it is two-tired.

Should a pregnant woman worry if her
baby is too hot?
**No, because it's always at womb
temperature.**

Did you hear about the cat who
swallowed a ball of yarn?
She had a litter of mittens.

Leather is perfect for sneaking around
because it's **literally made of hide**.

Scary monsters aren't very good at math, **unless you Count Dracula.**

I'm allergic to green onions. Every time I eat them, **I break out in chives.**

What do you call a camel with no humps?
Humphrey.

If dogs could have a profession, what would they be?
Roofers!

I was accused of being a plagiarist.
Their word, not mine!

What kind of things does a farmer talk about when he is milking cows?
Udder nonsense!

What does a marching band member use to brush his teeth?
A tuba toothpaste!

Dad: People keep accidentally asking me to purchase meat for them.
Son: By mistake?
Dad: Oh no, not you too!!

What word starts with "e", ends with "e", and only has one letter in it?
Envelope.

I taught my son how to use the word "abundance" in a sentence. He said, **"Thanks, dad, that really means a lot!"**

How do you make a water bed more bouncy?
Add spring water.

I really want to buy a step ladder but **I'm a little short.**

What do you call a zombie that writes music?
A decomposer.

My little sister just discovered she loves the poetry of Edgar Allan Poe.
She literally can't stop raven about it.

Ladies, if your boyfriend can't appreciate your fruit jokes, **you need to let that mango.**

What kind of salad can sink a ship?
One made with iceberg lettuce.

I'd rather not hear your story about Japanese sword fighters. **Can you just samurais it for me?**

After eating the ship, the sea monster said, **"I can't believe I ate the hull thing."**

What language do waterfowl speak? **Portu-geese.**

It used to be free to fill your car tire up with air. Now it coasts a dollar. **You know why? Inflation.**

What's a shark's favorite game?
Swallow the leader.

What type of fruit has to get married
with family and friends present?
A cantaloupe.

Why did the girl quit her job at the
doughnut factory?
**She was fed up with the hole
business.**

What do you call a bakery that has
burned down?
Toast.

Why is the scarecrow good at his job?
Hay. It's in his jeans!

What's a thief's favorite type of metal?
Steel.

If a country's main source of income is through horse sales **then it has a stable economy.**

I went to the zoo yesterday and saw a baguette in a cage. **The zookeeper said it was bread in captivity.**

Desi wants to add moisture to his shoebox, **but desiccant.**

What would be a great prison nickname?
"Mitochondria" because it's the powerhouse of a cell.

What is a pig's guitar made of?
Hamstrings!

What do they call the best salesman at a funeral home?
The Top Urner.

Can I make puns about Mediterranean islands?
Of Corsican, don't be Sicily!

How long should a jousting game last?
Until knight fall.

I wanted to see if my ten jokes passed the dad joke test, **but no pun in ten did.**

What does Geronimo say when he jumps out of an airplane?
"Meeeeeeeeeeeeeeeeeeee!"

What do you call a person who lives in Sweden but isn't from there?
An artificial Swedener.

Justice is a dish best served cold.
If it were served warm it would be just water.

What do you call an escaped prisoner camping in the woods?
Criminal in tent.

Did you hear about the guy who got hit in the head with a can of soda?
He's alright, it was a soft drink.

My brother couldn't afford to pay his water bill, so I mailed him a **"get well soon" card.**

I'd like to tell a joke about salt...**NA.** The guy at the tuxedo store kept hovering around me, so I asked him to leave me alone.
"Fine, suit yourself," he said.

What kind of fire leaves a room damp?
A humidi-fire.

What do you call a baby monkey?
A chimp off the old block.

A vegan said to me, "People who sell meat are disgusting!"
But actually, people who sell vegetables are grocer.

What did the Italian geometry teacher say when his house was robbed?
"What the hexagon?"

I was fired from the keyboard factory today because **I wasn't putting in enough shifts**.

I took a selfie after my kidney removal surgery. **#nofilter!**

I'm friends with 25 letters of the alphabet **and I don't know why.**

You know what **I've always said about suspense ....**

Why do bees stay in the hive during winter?
Swarm.

What do you call a hot dog race?
Wiener takes all.

What did the caveman say when the
big cat scratched him?
"Me ow."

What do you call an ape who likes to
touch people?
Chimp-handsy.

How do you know when you're caught
in freezing rain?
It hurts like hail.

I was going to sell my Chewbacca
cookies at the bake sale.
But they were all a little Chewy.

Did you know there was a knight who always gave up during battle?
His name was Sir Render.

I hate those people who knock on your door and tell you need to get "saved" or you'll "burn".
Crazy firemen.

How do you get two peaches to fight?
Pit them against each other!

My wife hates it when I mess with her red wine. **I added some fruit and now she's sangria than ever.**

Did you hear the joke about the statistician?
Probably.

69 and 70 got into a fight.
71.

Two guys were on a boat with three cigarettes and nothing to light them with. So they threw one overboard and the **boat became a cigarette lighter.**

What are a communist's favorite units of time?
Hours.

You can actually tell the gender of an ant by dropping it in water.
If it floats, it's boy ant.

Everyone talks about Murphy's Law, but I prefer Cole's law.
Especially when the cabbage is thinly sliced.

What do you get when you cross a turtle and a porcupine?
A slow poke!

Where did the Swedish cross country race end?
The Finnish line.

Why don't black holes have friends?
Because they a void.

How do you put a baby astronaut to sleep?
You rocket.

What did Pinocchio say to his barber?
"Just take a whittle off the top!"

I was never good at telling dad jokes.
Probably because he often worked late.

I bought a horse named mayo and **sometimes mayonnaise.**

What do you call a man on the floor of a hair salon?
Harry.

What do you call a sleeping policeman? **An under-covers cop.**

What do you call a skilled bird?
Talon-ted.

Two wrongs don't make a right, **but two Wrights do make an airplane.**

What do you call a priest who becomes a lawyer?
Father-in-law.

I don't like to brag about how all my friends let me borrow their brass instruments. **I just don't feel like tooting my own horn.**

What glove size does a psychic wear?
Medium.

There are two kinds of people in this world: **those who do things halfway, and…**

How do you fix a broken tomato?
Tomato paste!

Did you know the first French fries weren't cooked in France?
They were cooked in Greece.

What has 4 letters, sometimes has 9 letters, but never has 5 letters.

I went outside and saw a bird of prey with his MacBook eating avocado toast.
It was a millennial falcon.

Did you hear the one about the two cellmates?
They've been together for so long they're finishing each other's sentences.

Son: Dad, can you take my temperature?
Dad: Nah, you should just keep it.

Did you hear about the astronaut who stepped on chewing gum?
He got stuck in Orbit.

What do you call a vegetable that's standing in line?
A Queuecumber.

Did you hear about the cheese factory that exploded in France?
There was nothing left but de Brie.

People don't realize the health benefits of sun-dried grapes, **so I'm going to start raisin awareness.**

What happened when the cannibal showed up late to dinner?
His friends gave him the cold shoulder.

If you need to start a fire by rubbing two sticks together, make sure they're the same.
Then you'll have a match!

If you ever need an ark to save two of every animal, **I Noah guy**.

Digging holes can be fun,
but I simply find it boring!

Spent $500 for a limo, but I didn't get a driver for it.
All that money and nothing to chauffeur it.

My mayonnaise is trying kill me, **or so my sauces tell me.**

Who is the patron saint of email?
Saint Francis of a cc.

My grandfather has the odd habit of naming all the fish he catches.
Yesterday, he scaled Mount Everest.

What happened when the man tried
some bear stew?
He found it a bit grizzly.

How do you know when you've found a
good barista?
She makes a latte good tips.

Why was the Blarney Stone angry?
He was taken for granite.

When I stay in Italy,
I really like to Rome around.

How many moody teenagers does it take to screw in a light bulb?
Whatever!

I once spotted an albino leopard.
It was the least I could do.

Why are curious people so good at singing?
Because they inquire.

I have a great joke about time travel.
But you didn't get it.

What do Stormtroopers and churches
have in common?
Pew-pew-pew-pew-pew-pew!

Why was the army so strict about its
dress code?
To minimize casual tees.

Dad: Son, how can I stop my dad
jokes?
Son: Whatever means necessary!
Dad: Ha, no it doesn't!

Made in the USA
San Bernardino, CA
13 March 2020